WELCOME TO MS.BEE ABC'S

To order additional copies of this book, contact:
Xlibris
844-714-8691
www.Xlibris.com
Orders@Xlibris.com

ISBN: Softcover   978-1-6698-3506-6
             EBook   978-1-6698-3505-9

Print information available on the last page

Rev. date: 07/30/2022

WELCOME TO MS.BEE ABC'S

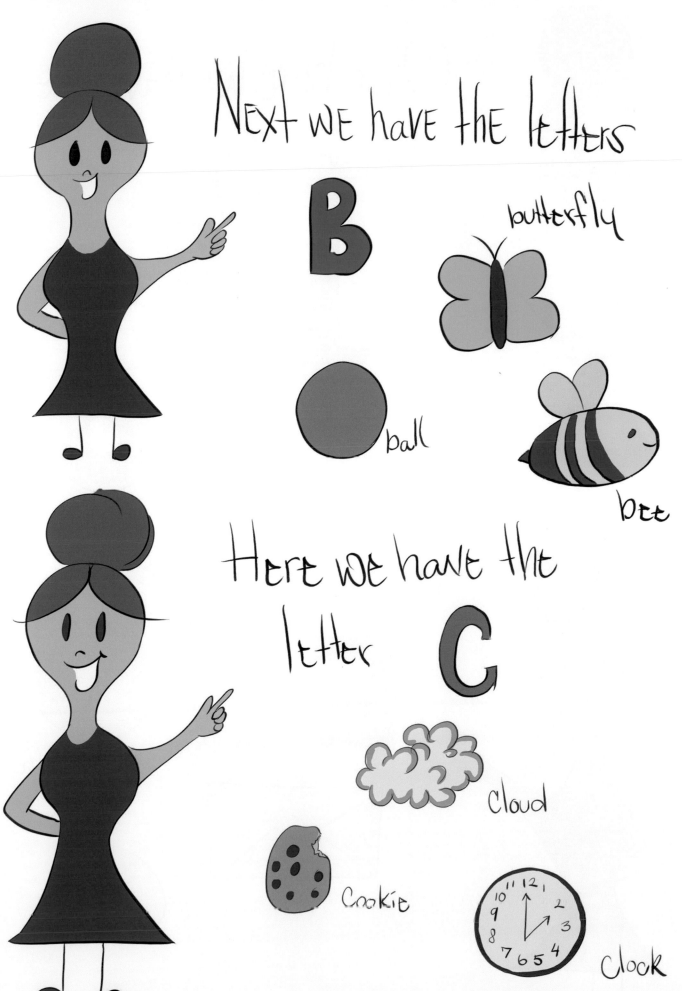

Next we have the letters

B

butterfly

ball

bee

Here we have the letter C

cloud

cookie

clock

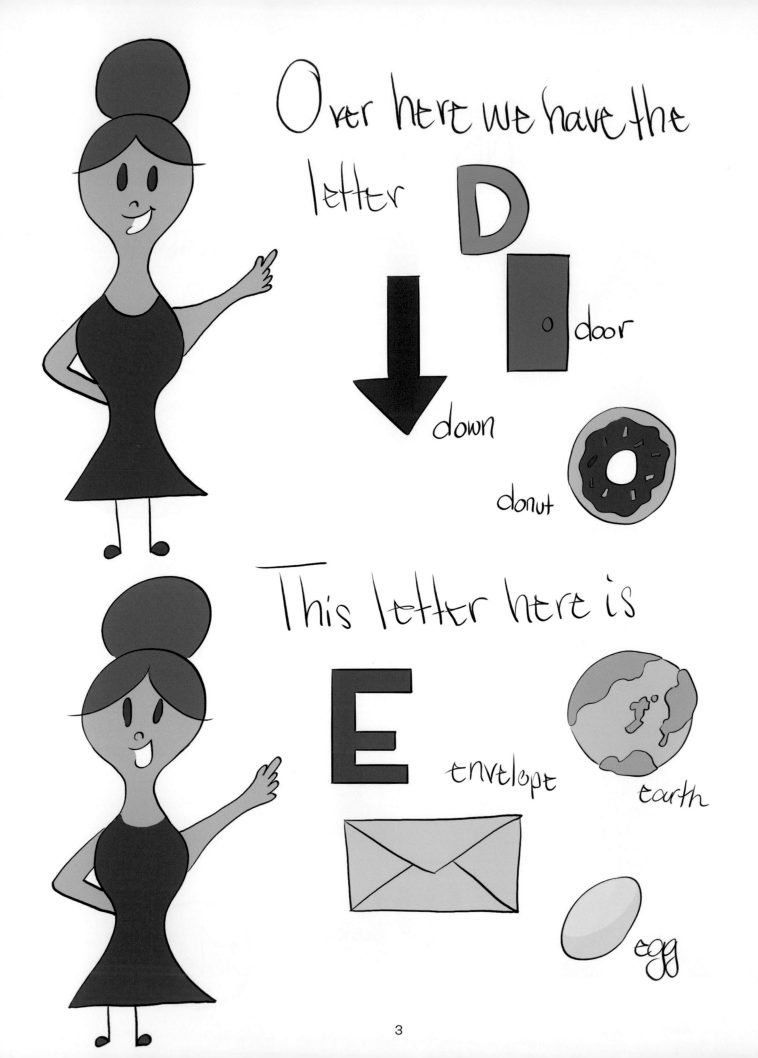

Over here we have the letter **D**

down

o door

donut

This letter here is **E**

envelope

earth

egg

This letter is

F

finger

flower

frits

Here we have the letter

G

glue

gift

glass

Over here we have

H

♥ heart

hand   house

This here is

I

icecube

island

ice cream

Next we have

J

Jam

Jar

Jug

This letter here is

K

Key

Kite

Kiel

This letter here is

L

lamp

lollipop

leaf

This here is

M

magic

mail

maracas

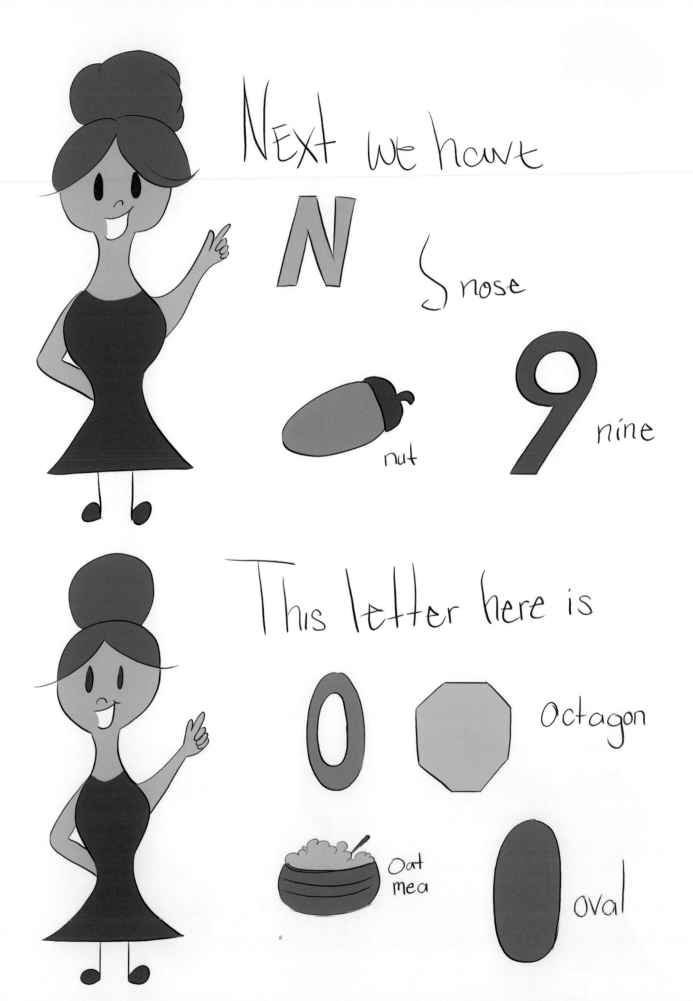

Next we have

N

S nose

nut

9 nine

This letter here is

O

Octagon

Oat mea

oval

Next we have

P

pizza

pincel

paint

This letter here

is Q

? question

quarter

quilt

This letter here is R

rain

ring

rug

This here is S

sun

Star

sword

Next we have

T 10 ten

tree 20 twenty

This letter here is

U umbrella

unhappy

This letterhere is

V

vine

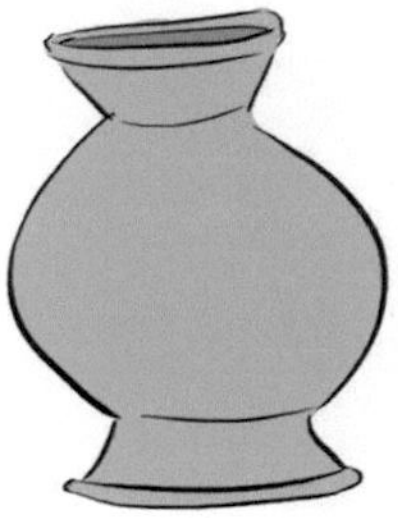

vase

vest

This letterhere

is W

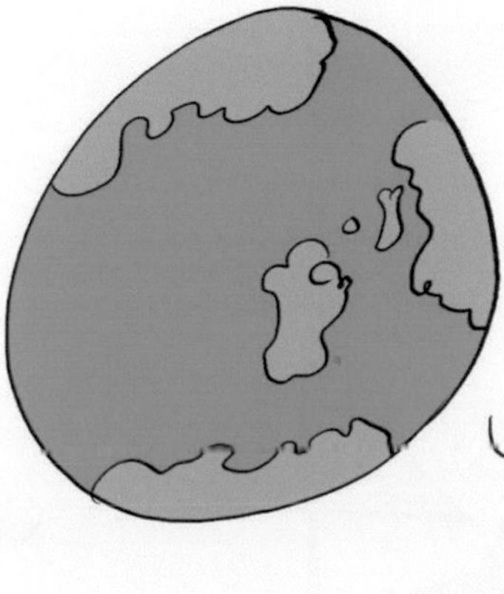

world

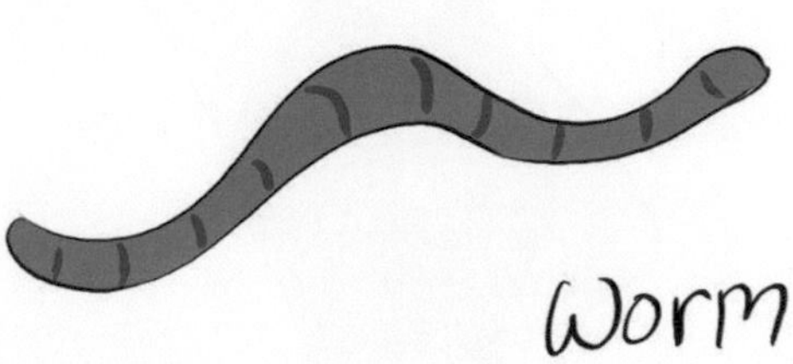

worm

wind

12

Now we have

X

X ray fish

xylophone

This letter here is

Y

yolk

yacht

yo yo

13

Lastly we have the letter

Z

zipper

zucchini

zero

Printed in the United States
by Baker & Taylor Publisher Services